Head Down

Balls Up!

Why It's your fault your business can't grow...

By Simon Ellson

Simon has won 7 consecutive awards for best client results, voted by his clients, in the largest coaching community in the UK, a testament to the power of coaching and positive feedback.

Photography courtesy of Beth Gregory at Folio Creative Co. Dorchester.

CONTENTS:

INTRODUCTION:

THE JOURNEY OF SELF-SABOTAGE

Let's cut straight to the chase >80% of business owners I meet are their own worst enemies. Yes, you read that right. Most of you reading this are probably doing everything you can to sabotage the very business you're working so hard to build. How do I know? Because I've been there, and I see it every day in business owners who are so **head down (working all those hours), balls up, (making mistakes right left and centre)** that they're practically digging their graves with a to-do list.

What's worse is that we think we're the exception. We believe we're grinding it out for some noble reason—providing for our families, building an empire, or some other heroic nonsense. But let's face it: half of the time we're just making busy work so we don't have to deal with the uncomfortable reality that we're avoiding the real hard stuff. The decisions that move the needle. The strategies that scale. The things that will get the business working *without us.*

Here's the truth, and brace yourself, because this might sting: you are probably the biggest roadblock in your own business. Yes, you. Not the economy, not your team, not the competition. It's you. And until you get your head out of the weeds, stop self-sabotaging, and start thinking like a real business owner instead of a firefighter, you're going to stay stuck. No matter how many hours you grind, how many motivational quotes you post, or how many times you listen to that one business podcast.

This book is going to slap you around a bit (figuratively speaking of course) and shake up your perspective. You'll recognise some familiar behaviours—procrastination, perfectionism, overthinking—all the usual suspects in your mental sabotage library. But the good news? By the end of this book, you'll have the tools to get out of your own way and build a business that works without you. Imagine that!

So put that seat belt on. As I said this might sting a little, but I promise it's for your own good. I'll repeat, I estimate that >80% of business owners are the biggest obstacles to their success. It's a startling thought, isn't it? Think about it: every morning, thousands of entrepreneurs wake up ready to tackle the day, only to find themselves tangled in the same traps they set for themselves the previous day.

You might be thinking, "That's not me," but have you ever found yourself so buried in work that you can't see the bigger picture? That's the moment when "head down" becomes less of a strategy and more of a "balls up" error strewn downfall.

Imagine this: you're in a room filled with business owners—ambitious, driven, and all working tirelessly to achieve success. I ask them one question: "How many of you believe your business could run smoothly without you for a month?" A few hands go up hesitantly, but most remain firmly in their laps. Why? Because despite all the hard work, most business owners unknowingly sabotage their freedom.

Only a staggering 4% of businesses in the UK make it over £1m pa in turnover and only 0.4% over £10m. Yes, you read that right, just 4%. If you are in that club congratulations! If you are not but want to be, read on...

Many of those other business owners are trapped in a cycle where they become the very reason their businesses can't function independently. It's not due to a lack of passion, knowledge, or even effort—it's often because they've spent years in "head down, balls up" mode, missing the point where they should have let go.

The irony? In the pursuit of building a self-sustaining business, they've built a prison instead.

Pain Points:

Let's get down to it for a moment. You're probably wearing every hat imaginable. You're the CEO, the head of sales, the HR department, the janitor—everything. You've been conditioned to believe that the more you do, the more successful your business will be. But here's the harsh truth: you're suffocating your own business by trying to do it all. Have you ever felt that no one can do things as well as you? That the minute you step away, things start to fall apart?

You're constantly firefighting, jumping from one crisis to the next, and it's exhausting.

The freedom you envisioned when you started your business feels like a distant dream. Your work-life balance is non-existent, your family and personal life are taking a backseat, and even when you're physically present, your mind is always at the office. Deep down, you know something's got to give. But instead of taking a step back and recalibrating, you double down. More hours, more control, more of the same. And yet, the business still demands more of you.

The reality is that the very habits and mindsets that made you a successful business owner are now the chains that are holding you and your business hostage.

The Vicious Cycle:

The root of this self-sabotage often lies in the stories we've been told about what it means to be a successful business owner. All those darned influencers that glorify the "hustle"—the long hours, the constant grind, the idea that if you're not working yourself to the bone, you're not doing enough. But this mindset is a trap. It convinces you that the only way to succeed is to be everywhere, do everything, and control every aspect of your business. You become the hero in your own story—the one who saves the day solves every problem and never takes a break. But heroes get tired. And when the hero is exhausted, who saves the business?

This is the cycle of self-sabotage that most business owners find themselves in. By being the indispensable linchpin of your business, you've inadvertently created a scenario where the business can't thrive without you. It's a vicious circle: the more you intervene, the more your team relies on you, and the more the business depends on your presence. The result? A business that isn't truly a business at all—it's a demanding job you can't quit.

My Promise:

Here's the good news: it doesn't have to be this way. This book is not about adding more to your already overflowing plate. It's about clearing the clutter and addressing the real issues that keep you chained to your business. It's about identifying the self-sabotaging behaviours that are holding you back and learning to replace them with strategies that will empower both you and your team.

We'll dive deep into the psychology of why business owners fall into this trap, uncovering the fears, habits, and misconceptions that fuel this cycle. More importantly, this book offers a roadmap to transformation.

You'll discover how to step back without things falling apart, how to build a team that can take the reins, and how to create systems that allow the business to run without you constantly at the helm.

By the end of this book, you'll not only understand why you've been standing in your own way, but you'll also have the tools to step aside and let your business flourish.

The Journey:

We'll start by tackling the foundational mindsets that lead to self-sabotage. We'll explore the 'Owner's Trap,' where business owners become the central bottleneck, and examine why letting go is often the hardest but most crucial step. Each chapter will delve into a specific aspect of this transformation: from developing leadership and trust within your team to implementing processes that allow the business to function autonomously.

We'll dissect real-world example case studies of business owners who faced the same challenges and successfully transitioned from being the linchpin to being the visionary. This book will guide you through the practical steps needed to break free from the "head down, balls up" mentality and shift toward a business model that offers both freedom and profitability. It's not about doing more; it's about doing things differently.

We'll explore strategies that range from mindset shifts to tactical business practices, covering topics like delegation, building a high-performing team, creating scalable processes, and setting boundaries that protect your time and energy. You'll learn how to empower others within your business to take ownership, so you're not the only one shouldering the burden. And for those who fear that stepping back means losing control, we'll address that head-on, showing you how the right systems can give you more control—by not having to control everything.

The Emotional Rollercoaster:

Stepping back is not just a strategic move; it's an emotional journey. For many, the business is an extension of their identity. You've poured your heart, soul, and countless hours into building it. The thought of handing over control can be terrifying. What if things go wrong? What if your team makes mistakes? What if the business fails without your constant oversight?

These are real fears, and this book won't shy away from addressing them. We'll delve into the emotional side of this transition—the fears, the doubts, and even the guilt that comes with stepping back. You'll learn how to overcome these emotional barriers and build a mindset that supports a healthier, more sustainable way of running your business. By the end of this book, you'll have not just the practical tools, but also the emotional resilience to let your business grow beyond you.

Why:

I've wanted to write this book for ages, why? because the definition of success is not being the hardest worker in the room; it's about building something that can thrive without your constant intervention. It's about reclaiming your time, your energy, and your life.

This book is intended to be a wake-up call. It's a challenge to rethink the way you've been operating and to consider that the very things you're doing to "save" or "build" your business might be what's holding it back.

If you're ready to break free from the self-imposed chains of self-sabotage, to build a business that not only survives but thrives without you, then it's time to turn the page and get stuck in.

The journey won't be easy, it never is, but you can’t climb a mountain without climbing a mountain. Are you choosing to be stuck exactly where you are?

So, let's embark on this path together and create a business that truly works—so you don’t have to, it’s your choice to make.

Choice and not chance determines your business and your life, so make a choice today

---

CHAPTER 1:

THE SABOTEUR WITHIN – RECOGNISING SELF-SABOTAGE

What is Self-Sabotage?

Every business owner has, at one point or another, been their own worst enemy. Whether it's getting stuck in the minutiae, doubting every decision, or taking on too much, these actions often stem from one root cause: self-sabotage. This silent saboteur manifests in many forms, such as overworking, procrastination, fear of success, or the classic impostor syndrome. At its core, self-sabotage is the gap between intention and action. You have the intention to grow your business, but your actions—or lack thereof—pull you in the opposite direction. It's as if you're driving with one foot on the accelerator and the other on the brake.

Self-sabotage often arises from deeply ingrained beliefs that we've developed over time. These beliefs shape our actions and reactions, frequently without us even realising it. Perhaps you believe that success requires relentless hard work, leading you to overextend yourself to the point of burnout. Or maybe you fear that success will come with responsibilities you're not ready for, causing you to unconsciously avoid growth opportunities.

Why Do Business Owners Self-Sabotage?

The psychology behind self-sabotage is complex. Often, it ties back to fear. The fear of failure is one of the most common culprits. Many business owners fear that taking risks or delegating tasks might lead to mistakes, financial losses, or a tarnished reputation. This fear keeps them stuck in their comfort zone, repeating familiar patterns even when they're not effective.

On the flip side, there's the fear of success. Yes, you heard that right—success can be just as daunting as failure. Some business owners fear the increased expectations and pressures that come with growth. They worry that achieving success will mean sacrificing their time, taking on new challenges they're unprepared for, or changing their current lifestyle. This fear can cause them to unknowingly sabotage their progress, keeping their business in a state of perpetual stagnation.

Impostor syndrome is another sneaky form of self-sabotage. Despite outward signs of success, many business owners struggle with the feeling that they're not truly competent. They worry that they're one mistake away from being "found out" as a fraud. This mindset leads to overcompensation—working longer hours, avoiding delegation, and hesitating to pursue new opportunities.

The Impact on Business Performance

Self-sabotage has a tangible impact on business performance. When you're stuck in this cycle, it can lead to poor decision-making, missed opportunities, and even a toxic work environment. You might find yourself constantly firefighting, dealing with the same problems repeatedly because you're not addressing the root cause. This not only drains your energy but also hinders your ability to think strategically and plan for the future.

Don’t forget that self-sabotage affects team morale. When employees see a leader who is overworked, stressed, and unwilling to delegate, it sends a message that the business is not operating at its best. Talented employees may feel undervalued or become disengaged, leading to high turnover rates and a lack of innovation.

Financially, the cost of self-sabotage can be staggering. Missed opportunities, inefficiencies, and poor team dynamics directly impact the bottom line. Many businesses plateau or even decline because the owner cannot get out of their own way. Without recognising and addressing these self-imposed barriers, long-term success remains elusive.

Recognising the Signs of Self-Sabotage

So, how do you know if you're sabotaging yourself? The first step is to look for patterns. Here are some common signs:

- Constant Firefighting: You’re always putting out fires but never solving the underlying issues.

- Micromanagement: You have difficulty trusting others to do the job right, so you end up doing everything yourself.

- Avoidance: You delay making crucial decisions, whether it’s hiring new staff, launching a new product, or investing in marketing.

- Burnout: You’re working long hours, yet your business isn’t progressing as it should.

- Lack of Clear Goals: You're busy, but no clear direction or strategy is guiding your efforts.

If any of these resonate with you, it's a strong indication that self-sabotage is at play. Recognising these behaviours is crucial because you can't change what you don't acknowledge.

The Cost of Not Addressing Self-Sabotage

Ignoring self-sabotage has long-term consequences. Your business may reach a point where growth stalls, and no matter how hard you work, it feels like you're spinning your wheels. You might even start to resent the very business you once loved. Financially, the cost can be steep. Opportunities for expansion, partnerships, or increased profitability pass by because you're too entrenched in your current patterns to seize them.

More importantly, unchecked self-sabotage can lead to burnout. When the business relies entirely on you and you're constantly battling against your mindset, it becomes unsustainable. The risk of mental and physical exhaustion is real, and it can lead to a point where walking away seems like the only option.

Deep Dive into Self-Sabotage Types

To understand how self-sabotage affects your business, let's explore some common types in more depth:

1. Procrastination: You know you need to tackle a challenging task or make a difficult decision, but you keep putting it off. Procrastination is often rooted in fear—fear of

failure, fear of making the wrong choice, or even fear of success. This delay creates a bottleneck in your business, preventing progress and growth.

2. Perfectionism: You strive for perfection in every aspect of your business, from the smallest detail to the biggest project. While high standards are admirable, perfectionism can lead to paralysis. You spend excessive time tweaking, refining, and revising, which prevents you from moving forward and achieving momentum.

3. Over-commitment: You say yes to every opportunity, every request, and every idea that comes your way. You believe that staying busy equates to being successful. However, over-commitment spreads you thin, reduces your effectiveness, and leads to burnout. You find yourself juggling too many tasks, unable to give any of them the attention they deserve.

Practical Exercise: Self-Sabotage Audit

Objective: To help you identify your self-sabotaging behaviours.

- Step 1: Reflect on the past six months. Write down instances where you felt overwhelmed, stuck, or frustrated in your business.

- Step 2: For each instance, ask yourself: "Was there a decision or action I avoided?" "Did my fear or self-doubt play a role in this situation?"

- Step 3: Identify any patterns in your responses. Highlight the top three recurring self-sabotaging behaviours.

- Step 4: Write a short action plan on how to address each of these behaviours in the upcoming month.

Deepening the Exercise:

- Step 5: Identify a trusted colleague, mentor, or business coach and discuss your findings with them. Sometimes, an external perspective can provide insights you might have overlooked.

- Step 6: Set a weekly check-in for the next month to track your progress. Reflect on the changes you've implemented and note any differences in your mindset and business performance.

Outcome:

By conducting this audit, you'll gain clarity on how your mindset might be holding your business back. This awareness is the first step toward breaking the cycle of self-sabotage.

Real-World Example: Jane's Catering Business

Jane owned a small but promising catering business. Despite the growing demand, she found herself constantly working late hours and declining new opportunities. She believed that if she didn't oversee every detail personally, the quality would drop, and her business would fail. This led to burnout and stagnation; her business couldn't grow beyond a certain point because she was the bottleneck.

Jane's Internal Struggle:

Jane feared that by delegating, she would lose control over the quality of her services. She felt that her business's reputation rested entirely on her shoulders, so she micromanaged every event, every dish, and every client interaction. Her fear of failure was so strong that it blinded her to the negative impact her actions were having on her business.

The Turning Point:

After a particularly exhausting month, Jane realised she was at a breaking point. She couldn't sustain this level of involvement without sacrificing her health and personal life. Reluctantly, she began to explore the idea of delegation. She started with small steps—assigning minor tasks to her team while maintaining oversight.

The Change:

Gradually, Jane discovered that her team was capable and even eager to take on more responsibility. By allowing them to handle the details, Jane was able to focus on strategic planning, marketing, and expanding her business's reach. She learned that delegation didn't mean losing control but rather empowering her team to contribute to the business's success. Over time, she shifted her role from the doer to the visionary, guiding the business's direction rather than getting lost in the day-to-day tasks.

Outcome:

Jane's business started to flourish. With a more balanced workload and a team that felt trusted and valued, her catering service could handle more clients and bigger events. Jane had broken the self-sabotage cycle and could finally see her business growing without her having to sacrifice her well-being.

Self-Reflection Questions

To further internalise the concepts in this chapter, take a moment to reflect on these questions:

- Do I often find myself overwhelmed and stuck in the same problems repeatedly?

- Am I avoiding making decisions that could move my business forward?

- How do I react to success? Does it make me uneasy or fearful?

- Am I holding on to tasks that I could delegate to others?

- Do I believe that my business can't succeed without my constant involvement?

Summary

Self-sabotage is the silent barrier that prevents many business owners from achieving their full potential. It manifests in various forms, from overworking to avoiding critical decisions. Recognising these behaviours is the first step toward creating a business that doesn't just work but thrives. By confronting the saboteur within, you lay the foundation for a business that can grow beyond your direct involvement, setting the stage for true freedom and success.

What you say to yourself,
about yourself when you are
by yourself becomes the truth!

CHAPTER 2:

THE ILLUSION OF CONTROL – MICROMANAGEMENT AND ITS PITFALLS

Overview

Micromanagement is a common pitfall for business owners and something I see regularly usually driven by the illusion of control. While keeping a close eye on every detail may seem like the best way to maintain quality, it often leads to burnout, stifles team creativity, and slows business growth. This chapter explores the roots of micromanagement, its detrimental effects on the business, and practical strategies to move away from this counterproductive behaviour.

What is Micromanagement?

- Micromanagement is an excessive need to control and oversee every aspect of a business. While attention to detail is important, micromanagement crosses the line into obsession. This behaviour can stem from various beliefs, such as "No one can do it better than I can" or "If I'm not involved, things will go wrong." These beliefs create an environment where the business owner becomes the bottleneck.

The Roots of Micromanagement

- Micromanagement often originates from fear—fear of mistakes, fear of losing control, and fear of letting others take the reins. Many business owners find comfort in the belief that their constant involvement ensures success. This illusion of control can lead to overwork and overwhelm, leaving the business owner perpetually tied to the day-to-day operations.

The Costs of Micromanagement

- On the Business: Micromanagement stifles innovation and slows down processes. When every decision must go through the owner, it creates a bottleneck, delaying important actions and reducing the business's ability to respond quickly to changes.

- On the Team: Employees working under a micromanaging leader often feel undervalued and distrusted. This environment hampers creativity, diminishes morale, and can lead to high staff turnover. Talented individuals want autonomy and room to grow; when they don't get it, they leave.

- On the Owner: The business owner becomes overwhelmed and trapped in the minutiae of operations. This not only leads to burnout but also prevents the owner from focusing on strategic growth and long-term vision.

Recognising Micromanagement in Yourself

- Signs of Micromanagement:

  - Reluctance to delegate tasks or projects.

  - Overly detailed involvement in team members' work.

  - Frequent checking and double-checking of others' tasks.

- Correcting or redoing work that has already been completed.

- Self-Assessment: Are you often frustrated because "nobody does it right"? Do you find yourself involved in tasks that should be handled by others? If so, you might be caught in the micromanagement trap.

Breaking Free from the Micromanagement Cycle

- Building Trust: The key to overcoming micromanagement is trust. This involves believing in the abilities of your team and allowing them the autonomy to do their jobs. Start small by delegating less critical tasks, then gradually increase as your comfort level grows.

- Setting Clear Expectations: Instead of hovering over every task, set clear expectations and outcomes for your team. Provide guidelines but allow them the freedom to choose how they reach those goals.

- Shifting to a Coaching Mindset: Transition from being a manager to a coach. Focus on guiding and developing your team rather than controlling every aspect of their work. Encourage problem-solving and support your team in making decisions.

Practical Exercise:

Micromanagement Detox

- Objective: To help you identify and start letting go of micromanagement tendencies.

- Step 1: Identify one area of your business that you frequently micromanage. This could be a specific task, project, or department.

- Step 2: For the next week, consciously step back from this area. Choose a trusted team member to take over the responsibilities and set clear expectations for the outcomes rather than the process.

- Step 3: Resist the urge to intervene unless absolutely necessary. Instead, schedule regular check-ins to discuss progress and offer support.

- Step 4: Reflect on the results at the end of the week. Did things fall apart without your constant oversight, or did they progress as expected? How did stepping back affect your workload and mindset?

- Outcome: This exercise aims to break the immediate need for control and demonstrate that the business can function—and even thrive—without the owner's constant involvement.

Real-World Example:

Example: Tom's IT Consulting Firm

Tom started his IT consulting firm with a clear vision and a strong technical background. As the business grew, he hired a small team but found it difficult to let go of the tasks he used to handle. He was constantly checking in on his employees, rewriting their reports, and micromanaging every client interaction. His team began to feel frustrated, and Tom found himself working longer hours than ever.

Tom's Internal Struggle:

Tom believed that the quality of the work would suffer without his direct involvement. He felt that his clients expected a certain standard that only he could deliver. This belief caused him to hover over every task, giving his team little room to innovate or grow.

The Turning Point:

Tom reached a point of exhaustion where he realised he could not sustain this level of involvement. A business mentor challenged him to identify the tasks he was micromanaging and step back from them. Tom decided to let his senior consultant handle a major project with minimal interference.

The Change:

To his surprise, the project was completed successfully. His senior consultant not only met the client's expectations but also introduced new efficiencies that Tom hadn't considered. This experience helped Tom realise that his team was capable and eager to contribute more. He began to delegate more effectively, providing clear expectations and outcomes without dictating every step of the process.

Outcome:

Tom's business became more agile and responsive. His team felt more empowered and motivated, which led to increased job satisfaction and reduced turnover. Tom regained his focus on strategic growth, leading to a 30% increase in revenue within a year. By overcoming his micromanagement tendencies, Tom was able to scale his business and create a more balanced work-life dynamic.

Self-Reflection Questions:

- Do I often feel that I need to oversee every aspect of my business to ensure success?

- How often do I find myself redoing tasks that others have completed?

- What tasks or projects am I currently micromanaging, and why?

- How does my involvement affect my team's morale and performance?

- What small steps can I take to start letting go of the need for constant control?

Summary

Micromanagement is a subtle form of self-sabotage that stems from the illusion of control. While it may offer a temporary sense of security, it ultimately hinders business growth, stifles team creativity, and leads to burnout. By recognising and addressing micromanagement tendencies, business owners can foster a more autonomous and innovative work environment. This, in turn, frees the owner to focus on strategic vision and long-term success, rather than being bogged down in daily operations.

If you micromanage tasks, you create resentment, if you delegate authority, you create trust!

Chapter 3:

Drowning in the Day-to-Day – The Lack of Strategic Planning

Overview

Many business owners find themselves drowning in the daily grind, constantly reacting to immediate issues rather than steering their business toward long-term goals. The lack of strategic planning is a form of self-sabotage that keeps owners trapped in a cycle of busyness without progress. In this chapter, we'll explore why strategic planning is often neglected, the consequences of operating without a plan, and how to break free by adopting a proactive approach.

What is Strategic Planning?

- Strategic planning involves setting long-term objectives and determining the best course of action to achieve them. It requires stepping back from daily operations to consider the bigger picture. Many business owners mistakenly believe they don't have the time for strategic planning, viewing it as a luxury rather than a necessity. However, without a clear plan, they end up reacting to circumstances rather than controlling their business's direction.

Why Do Business Owners Neglect Strategic Planning?

- Immediate Pressures: The day-to-day demands of running a business can be overwhelming. There are always fires to put out, from handling customer complaints to managing cash flow. These immediate pressures create an illusion of productivity, making it easy to deprioritise long-term planning.

- Fear of Uncertainty: Strategic planning involves looking into the future, which can be daunting. Many business owners fear making the wrong decisions or setting unrealistic goals, so they avoid planning altogether. They might also worry about committing to a path that requires change or risk.

- Lack of Knowledge: Some business owners simply don't know how to create an effective strategic plan. They may be experts in their field but lack the skills needed to analyse market trends, set realistic goals, and develop a roadmap for success.

The Consequences of Operating Without a Plan

- Reactive Business Culture: Without a strategic plan, the business operates in a reactive mode, constantly responding to external pressures rather than proactively shaping its future. This leads to inconsistency, missed opportunities, and a lack of direction for the team.

- Stagnation: A lack of strategic planning often results in stagnation. The business might perform adequately in the short term but fails to evolve or grow. Over time, competitors with a clear vision and plan will outpace the business, leaving it behind.

- Burnout for the Owner: When the business owner is trapped in the day-to-day grind, they have no time or energy to think strategically. This not only hampers the business's growth but also leads to burnout. The owner becomes the bottleneck, unable to delegate or focus on higher-level decisions.

Shifting from Reactive to Proactive

- Creating Time for Planning: Strategic planning doesn't happen by accident; it requires a conscious effort to carve out time from the daily routine. This means prioritising planning sessions and treating them as non-negotiable commitments. It might involve setting aside a day each quarter to step back and evaluate the business's direction.

- Setting Clear, Measurable Goals: Strategic planning starts with defining clear, long-term goals. These goals should be specific, measurable, achievable, relevant, and time-bound (SMART). They serve as the North Star that guides all business decisions and actions.

- Developing an Actionable Roadmap: A strategic plan is not a wish list; it's a detailed roadmap that outlines the steps needed to reach the desired goals. This involves breaking down long-term objectives into smaller, manageable tasks and setting milestones to track progress.

Practical Exercise:

Strategic Planning Starter Kit

- Objective: To initiate the strategic planning process and identify key goals for your business.

- Step 1: Schedule a strategic planning session. Block out at least half a day where you can focus solely on this exercise without distractions.

- Step 2: Conduct a SWOT Analysis (Strengths, Weaknesses, Opportunities, Threats). Write down your business's internal strengths and weaknesses, as well as external opportunities and threats in the market.

- Step 3: Define 3-5 long-term goals for your business (over 3-5 years). Ensure these goals are SMART—specific, measurable, achievable, relevant, and time-bound.

- Step 4: Break down each goal into actionable steps. Identify what needs to be done in the next year, six months, and quarter to move closer to each goal.

- Step 5: Set milestones and assign responsibilities. Determine who will be responsible for each task and set deadlines for completion.

- Outcome: This exercise provides a starting point for strategic planning, shifting your focus from daily firefighting to long-term growth and direction.

Real-World Example:

Example: Sarah's Boutique Fitness Studio

Sarah owned a boutique fitness studio that was doing well in terms of customer satisfaction but wasn't growing. She spent most of her time teaching classes, handling client queries, and managing daily operations. The business was stable, but Sarah felt stuck and unable to take it to the next level.

Sarah's Internal Struggle:

Sarah feared that stepping back from the daily operations would lead to a decline in service quality. She was also overwhelmed by the idea of strategic planning. The thought of looking five years into the future seemed daunting, and she didn't know where to start. As a result, she kept putting it off, believing she'd get to it "someday."

The Turning Point:

After attending a business workshop, Sarah realised that her lack of planning was the very thing holding her back. She decided to set aside one day each quarter to focus on strategic planning. She began with a SWOT analysis to understand her studio's position in the market and identify areas for growth.

The Change:

Sarah identified key opportunities, such as expanding her class offerings and launching an online fitness program. She set clear goals, including increasing her customer base by 20% and developing a new revenue stream through online classes. By breaking these goals into actionable steps, she was able to delegate daily tasks to her staff, freeing up her time for strategic initiatives.

Outcome:

Within a year, Sarah's studio experienced significant growth. The new online program attracted clients from outside her local area, providing a steady stream of additional income. By focusing on strategic planning, Sarah transformed her business from a stable but stagnant operation into a dynamic, growing enterprise.

Self-Reflection Questions:

- How much time do I currently spend on strategic planning versus daily operations?

- What are my long-term goals for my business, and have I clearly defined them?

- Do I have a roadmap to achieve these goals, or am I simply reacting to daily demands?

- What immediate steps can I take to start prioritising strategic planning?

- How can I delegate or streamline daily tasks to free up time for planning?

Summary

A lack of strategic planning is a major form of self-sabotage that keeps business owners trapped in the day-to-day grind.

Without a clear plan, the business drifts aimlessly, reacting to circumstances rather than shaping its future.

By consciously shifting from a reactive to a proactive mindset, business owners can set a clear direction for growth, making informed decisions that align with their long-term vision.

Strategic planning is not a one-time event but an ongoing process that requires commitment and focus. The rewards are a business that thrives with a clear sense of purpose and direction.

There are dreamers and there are planners; Planners make their dreams come true

---

CHAPTER 4:

FEAR OF LETTING GO – DELEGATION DILEMMAS

Overview

Delegation is a critical skill for any business owner aiming to build a self-sustaining business. However, many struggle with the fear of letting go, leading to a reluctance to delegate essential tasks. This chapter dives into the roots of this fear, the negative impact of poor delegation on business growth, and practical strategies to overcome the barriers to effective delegation.

Understanding the Fear of Letting Go

- The fear of letting go is common among business owners who equate their business's success with their direct involvement. This mindset creates a cycle where the owner becomes the primary bottleneck. The underlying belief is often, "If I don't do it, it won't be done right." This fear stems from various sources:

- Control: The desire to maintain control over every aspect of the business, fearing that others won't meet the same standards.

- Perfectionism: The belief that no one else can execute tasks with the same level of precision or care.

- Trust Issues: A lack of trust in others' abilities, often because of past experiences where delegation resulted in mistakes or failures.

The Consequences of Not Delegating

- Owner Burnout: When the business owner tries to handle everything, it inevitably leads to burnout. The constant juggling of tasks prevents them from focusing on strategic initiatives and big-picture growth.

- Stifled Business Growth: When every decision and task relies on the owner, the business hits a ceiling. There's only so much one person can do in a day, which limits scalability and prevents the business from reaching its full potential.

- Team Disengagement: Employees who feel undervalued or underutilised become disengaged. They may feel they're not trusted with important responsibilities, leading to a lack of motivation and creativity. This can result in high turnover rates and a loss of talent.

The Benefits of Effective Delegation

- Increased Capacity: Delegating frees up the owner's time to focus on strategic planning, innovation, and activities that drive long-term growth.

- Empowered Team: When employees are trusted with meaningful tasks, they feel valued and motivated. This empowerment leads to higher job satisfaction, increased productivity, and a culture of accountability.

- Better Decision-Making: Delegation allows for diverse perspectives in decision-making. Team members bring unique skills and insights that can lead to more informed and innovative solutions.

Overcoming the Barriers to Delegation

- Shift in Mindset: Delegation is not about handing off tasks to be rid of them; it's about entrusting others with the responsibility to leverage their strengths. Understand that mistakes are a part of growth and that others can bring fresh perspectives and skills to the table.

- Start Small: Begin by delegating less critical tasks that don't require your direct involvement. This could be administrative tasks, routine customer communications, or smaller projects. As you become more comfortable, gradually delegate more significant responsibilities.

- Set Clear Expectations: Effective delegation requires clarity. When assigning a task, clearly communicate the desired outcome, any key parameters, and the level of autonomy the individual has. Be available for support but resist the urge to micromanage.

- Build Trust: Trust is built through consistent, positive experiences. Give your team the opportunity to prove themselves. Acknowledge their efforts and provide constructive feedback to foster an environment of growth and collaboration.

Practical Exercise:

Delegation Development Plan

- Objective: To practice and improve your delegation skills by gradually transferring responsibilities to your team.

- Step 1: Identify three tasks or responsibilities that you currently handle but could potentially delegate. List them in order of complexity.

- Step 2: For each task, identify a team member who could take it on. Consider their strengths, skills, and current workload.

- Step 3: Create a clear outline for each task, including the expected outcome, any critical parameters, and the deadline. Set a time for an initial briefing with the selected team member.

- Step 4: During the briefing, communicate your expectations clearly and encourage questions. Provide them with the necessary resources and authority to complete the task.

- Step 5: Schedule regular check-ins to monitor progress, offer support, and provide feedback. Focus on guiding rather than controlling.

- Step 6: Reflect on the outcomes once each task is completed. What went well? Were there any challenges? How did the delegation affect your workload and stress levels?

- Outcome: This exercise helps you build confidence in your ability to delegate, supports team development, and provides a structured approach to gradually letting go of control.

Real-World Example:

Example: David's Marketing Agency

David owned a small but thriving marketing agency. As the business grew, he found himself overwhelmed with managing client accounts, creating marketing strategies, and handling administrative work. His reluctance to delegate was rooted in the fear that his clients would only receive the level of service they expected if he was directly involved.

David's Internal Struggle:

David believed that his personal touch was what set his agency apart. He feared that delegating tasks to his team would lead to a decline in quality and potentially damage the agency's reputation. This belief caused him to micromanage projects and become the bottleneck in the business, slowing down progress and exhausting himself.

The Turning Point:

After missing several important family events due to his workload, David realised that his current approach was unsustainable. He needed to trust his team if he wanted to create a more balanced life. He decided to start small by delegating the management of a few clients accounts to his senior staff.

The Change:

David chose two experienced account managers and provided them with detailed briefs on the clients. He communicated his expectations and gave them the autonomy to make decisions within agreed-upon parameters. David set up weekly check-ins to review the accounts' progress and offer support. To his surprise, the clients responded positively to the change. The account managers brought new ideas and strategies that improved client satisfaction and results.

Outcome:

By gradually delegating more responsibilities, David found that his team was not only capable but also brought fresh perspectives that enhanced the agency's services. His workload decreased significantly, allowing him to focus on strategic growth and business development. The agency continued to grow, and David was able to regain his work-life balance. By overcoming his fear of letting go, he transformed his business into a more dynamic and scalable operation.

Self-Reflection Questions:

- What tasks or responsibilities am I currently holding onto out of fear of letting go?

- How do my fears of delegation affect my workload and stress levels?

- What small steps can I take to start building trust in my team's abilities?

- How can I set clear expectations when delegating tasks to ensure successful outcomes?

- What impact could effective delegation have on my business growth and personal well-being?

Summary

The fear of letting go is a common form of self-sabotage that limits business growth and leads to burnout. Effective delegation is not about relinquishing control but about empowering others to contribute their skills and strengths to the business. By shifting your mindset, starting small, and setting clear expectations, you can overcome the barriers to delegation. This, in turn, frees up your time to focus on strategic initiatives, fosters a more engaged and productive team, and paves the way for a more scalable and sustainable business.

The real battle in life is
between hanging on and
letting go, its your choice!

CHAPTER 5:

PERFECTIONISM – WHEN GOOD ENOUGH IS BETTER

Overview

Perfectionism can be a hidden form of self-sabotage for business owners. While striving for excellence is admirable, the relentless pursuit of perfection often leads to paralysis, inefficiency, and missed opportunities. In this chapter, we'll explore the dangers of perfectionism, how it hampers business growth, and how to embrace a mindset where "good enough" is sometimes the key to progress.

Understanding Perfectionism in Business

- Perfectionism is the belief that anything less than perfect is unacceptable. In the context of business, this manifests as an excessive focus on details, endless tweaking of products or services, and a reluctance to launch or delegate until every element is flawless. While attention to detail is important, perfectionism crosses the line into counterproductive behaviour. It creates a mindset where progress is stalled in the pursuit of an unattainable ideal.

- Common Signs of Perfectionism:

  - Reluctance to delegate due to fear that others won't meet your standards.

  - Constantly revisiting projects, even after completion, to make minor adjustments.

- Delaying the launch of products or services because they're "not quite ready."

- Setting unrealistically high standards that lead to disappointment and burnout.

The Roots of Perfectionism

- Perfectionism often stems from deep-seated beliefs about self-worth, success, and failure. Many business owners hold themselves to impossibly high standards, believing that any mistake will lead to criticism or failure. This fear of being judged can create a paralysing effect, where the pursuit of perfection becomes a means of avoiding vulnerability. Additionally, perfectionism can be driven by a desire for control and a need to prove one's competence.

The Costs of Perfectionism

- Paralysis by Analysis: Perfectionism leads to over-analysis and over-planning, causing delays in decision-making and execution. Opportunities slip by because the owner is stuck in a cycle of endless revisions and tweaks.

- Inefficiency: The excessive time spent perfecting every detail results in inefficiencies and wasted resources. Rather than focusing on what moves the business forward, perfectionists get bogged down in minutiae that have little impact on the overall outcome.

- Burnout: The constant pressure to achieve perfection is exhausting. It leads to burnout, decreased productivity, and ultimately, dissatisfaction with the business. The joy and creativity that come from running a business are overshadowed by stress and frustration.

- Missed Opportunities: While the business owner is caught up in perfecting one aspect of their business, competitors who embrace a more agile approach may seize market opportunities and innovate faster.

Embracing the Concept of "Good Enough"

- Reframing Perfection: The key to overcoming perfectionism is to reframe your mindset. Recognise that in business, perfection is not only unattainable but also unnecessary. Customers do not expect perfection; they expect value, reliability, and responsiveness. Learn to differentiate between what is essential for success and what is merely a "nice to have."

- Focus on Progress, Not Perfection: Shift your focus from perfect outcomes to continuous improvement. Adopt a mindset of iteration, where you launch, learn, and refine. This approach not only accelerates progress but also fosters innovation and adaptability.

- Set Realistic Standards: Establish realistic standards that align with your business's goals and values. Aim for excellence where it matters most but allow flexibility and imperfection in less critical areas. Recognise that "good enough" is often a stepping stone to "great."

Strategies to Overcome Perfectionism

- Set Clear Priorities: Identify the core areas of your business that truly require excellence and allocate your efforts accordingly. For other areas, define what "good enough" looks like and to give yourself permission to move on once that standard is met.

- Implement Deadlines: Deadlines are an effective tool for curbing perfectionist tendencies. Commit to launching a product, service, or project by a specific date, even if it's not flawless. Deadlines force you to focus on what's essential and discourage endless tweaking.

- Seek Feedback Early: Rather than striving for perfection before releasing something, seek feedback early in the process. Engaging with customers, team members, or mentors can provide valuable insights and help you improve without obsessing over every detail.

- Practice Self-Compassion: Understand that mistakes and imperfections are part of the learning and growth process. Practice self-compassion by acknowledging your efforts and progress rather than fixating on perceived shortcomings.

Practical Exercise:

The 80/20 Perfectionism Challenge

- Objective: To identify areas where perfectionism is hindering progress and practice adopting a "good enough" mindset.

- Step 1: Identify a current project or task where you feel stuck due to perfectionism. This could be anything from finalising a new product to creating a marketing campaign.

- Step 2: Apply the 80/20 rule. Identify the 20% of elements that will contribute to 80% of the project's success. Focus your efforts on perfecting these key aspects.

- Step 3: Define what "good enough" looks like for the remaining 80% of the project. Set a clear, realistic standard and give yourself permission to accept this level of completion.

- Step 4: Set a deadline to complete the project, focusing on delivering value rather than perfection. Use this deadline to drive action and prevent overthinking.

- Step 5: Reflect on the outcome. Did the project meet its objectives? How did letting go of perfectionism impact your efficiency and stress levels?

- Outcome: This exercise helps you identify where perfectionism is holding you back and encourages a mindset shift toward prioritising progress and value over perfection.

Real-World Example:

Example: Lisa's Artisan Bakery

Lisa owned a small artisan bakery known for its high-quality, handmade goods. She had a loyal customer base and frequently received requests to expand her product line.

However, Lisa's perfectionism kept her from introducing new items. She spent months developing each product, tweaking recipes, and perfecting presentation. As a result, her product launches were infrequent, and she often missed out on seasonal market opportunities.

Lisa's Internal Struggle:

Lisa feared that releasing anything less than perfect would damage her bakery's reputation. She believed that every product had to be flawless to satisfy her customers and maintain her brand image. This mindset caused her to invest excessive time and resources into each product, leading to stress and burnout.

The Turning Point:

After attending a local business seminar, Lisa realised that her perfectionism was holding her business back. She decided to try a different approach by applying the 80/20 rule to her product development process. Instead of striving for perfection in every detail, she focused on perfecting the core elements that mattered most to her customers—taste and quality ingredients.

The Change:

Lisa set a deadline to launch a new line of seasonal pastries within a month. She involved her customers by seeking their feedback on prototypes and iterating based on their responses. The result was a successful product launch that was well-received by her customers. Although the pastries weren't perfect in Lisa's eyes, they delivered on taste and quality, which was what her customers valued most.

Outcome:

By embracing a "good enough" mindset, Lisa was able to introduce new products more frequently, keeping her bakery fresh and competitive. She learned that her customers appreciated the variety and innovation more than perfection in every detail. Her bakery's revenue grew, and Lisa experienced a renewed sense of creativity and enjoyment in her work. She realised that progress and customer value were more important than an unattainable standard of perfection.

Self-Reflection Questions:

- Where in my business am I striving for perfection at the expense of progress?

- How do my perfectionist tendencies affect my decision-making and productivity?

- What aspects of my business could benefit from an 80/20 approach?

- How can I redefine my standards to focus on delivering value rather than perfection?

- What steps can I take to practice self-compassion and embrace imperfection as part of the process?

Summary

Perfectionism, though often seen as a virtue, can be a significant form of self-sabotage that hinders business growth and innovation. The relentless pursuit of perfection leads to paralysis, inefficiency, and burnout.

By embracing a mindset where "good enough" is sometimes the key to progress, business owners can focus on delivering value, moving forward, and adapting to market needs. Overcoming perfectionism involves setting realistic standards, seeking feedback, and practising self-compassion.

This shift not only enhances efficiency and creativity but also fosters a more agile and resilient business.

Perfection is the enemy of good, so surely done is better than perfect?

CHAPTER 6:

THE BUSYNESS TRAP – MISTAKING ACTIVITY FOR PRODUCTIVITY

Overview

Many business owners fall into the busyness trap—confusing being busy with being productive. The daily grind of endless tasks can create an illusion of progress when, in reality, it might be hindering real growth and strategic development. In this chapter, we'll explore the difference between busyness and productivity, how this trap leads to self-sabotage, and how to focus on high-impact activities that drive meaningful results.

Understanding the Busyness Trap

- The busyness trap is the tendency to fill your day with tasks that keep you occupied but don't necessarily move your business forward. It's about being constantly in motion without making strategic progress. Busyness can feel rewarding because it creates a sense of accomplishment, yet it often leads to burnout without tangible results. The mantra of "staying busy" can blind business owners to the importance of prioritising tasks that align with their long-term goals.

Signs You're Stuck in the Busyness Trap:

- Your day is filled with meetings, emails, and minor tasks, leaving little time for strategic thinking.

- You constantly feel overwhelmed but can't identify what you've actually accomplished at the end of the day.

- You avoid larger, more important projects because they seem too time-consuming or daunting.

Why Business Owners Fall into the Trap

- Fear of Idleness: Many business owners equate busyness with success. They fear that slowing down or taking time to plan will lead to a loss of momentum or appear as laziness. This fear drives them to fill every moment with activity, even if it's not productive.

- Lack of Prioritisation: Without clear priorities, it's easy to get caught up in tasks that feel urgent but aren't important. The absence of a structured plan makes it challenging to distinguish between what truly needs attention and what can be delegated or postponed.

- The Illusion of Control: Staying busy can create an illusion of control over the business. Constant activity provides a sense of involvement and importance, making it difficult to step back and assess whether the efforts are genuinely productive.

The Cost of Busyness

- Burnout: Constant busyness leads to burnout. The relentless pursuit of ticking off tasks drains energy and enthusiasm, leaving little room for creativity or strategic thought. Over time, this can result in decreased productivity and even health issues.

- Missed Opportunities: By focusing on low-impact tasks, business owners miss out on opportunities that require strategic thinking and long-term planning. The busyness trap prevents them from identifying new growth areas, exploring innovative ideas, or building strategic partnerships.

- Stunted Growth: A business that operates on busyness rather than strategic productivity stagnates. Without focus on high-impact activities, growth plateaus, and the business becomes reactive rather than proactive, merely surviving instead of thriving.

Shifting from Busy to Productive

- Identify High-Impact Activities: High-impact activities are those that directly contribute to your long-term business goals. These include strategic planning, building key relationships, improving processes, and developing new products or services. Identifying these activities helps you focus on what truly matters.

- Adopt the 80/20 Rule: The Pareto Principle (80/20 rule) states that 80% of your results come from 20% of your efforts. Identify the 20% of activities that drive the most significant outcomes for your business and prioritise them. This shift in focus ensures that your efforts are aligned with your goals.

- Set Boundaries and Say No: Learning to say no to non-essential tasks is crucial. Set boundaries around your time and commitments. Avoid the temptation to fill your schedule with activities that do not contribute to your strategic objectives.

- Embrace Time Management Techniques: Time management tools like time blocking, prioritisation matrices, and the "two-minute rule" can help you allocate time more effectively. By organising your day around high-priority tasks, you can ensure that your busyness translates into productivity.

Practical Exercise:

The Productivity Audit

- Objective: To identify areas where you are mistaking busyness for productivity and refocus on high-impact activities.

- Step 1: Track your daily activities for one week. Use a notebook or digital tool to log every task you work on, including meetings, emails, and interruptions. Be specific about the time spent on each activity.

- Step 2: At the end of the week, categorise each activity using the Eisenhower Matrix:

  - Quadrant 1: Urgent and Important

  - Quadrant 2: Not Urgent but Important

  - Quadrant 3: Urgent but Not Important

  - Quadrant 4: Not Urgent and Not Important

- Step 3: Analyse your results. How much of your time was spent on high-impact activities (Quadrant 2)? Were you primarily occupied with Quadrant 3 and 4 tasks?

- Step 4: Identify the top 20% of activities (using the 80/20 rule) that had the most significant impact on your business. Plan to prioritise these activities moving forward.

- Step 5: Create an action plan to minimise or delegate low-impact tasks. Set aside dedicated time each week to focus on high-impact activities that align with your long-term goals.

- Outcome: This exercise helps you distinguish between being busy and being productive. By focusing on high-impact activities, you can make strategic progress rather than getting caught in the cycle of busyness.

Real-World Example:

Example: Mark's Consultancy Firm

Mark ran a consultancy firm that was moderately successful but not growing as he had hoped. His days were packed with back-to-back meetings, responding to emails, and handling client requests. He was always busy but felt like he wasn't making meaningful progress. Despite the hustle, his business growth remained stagnant.

Mark's Internal Struggle:

Mark equated busyness with success. He believed that being constantly occupied was a sign of a thriving business.

However, he also felt frustrated and exhausted, unsure why his endless efforts weren't translating into significant growth.

The Turning Point:

During a coaching session, Mark was challenged to audit his activities over a week. He discovered that the majority of his time was spent on low-impact tasks, such as administrative work and minor client issues, leaving little time for strategic planning or business development.

The Change:

Mark decided to implement the 80/20 rule. He identified the key activities that drove the most results, such as building strategic partnerships and developing new service offerings. He began delegating low-impact tasks to his team and set boundaries around his time. He also adopted time-blocking techniques to dedicate specific hours to high-impact activities.

Outcome:

Within a few months, Mark noticed a shift in his business. By focusing on high-impact activities, he was able to launch a new service line, attracting larger clients and increasing revenue. His workdays became more structured, reducing his stress levels and providing a clearer sense of direction. Mark learned that true productivity came from strategic action, not just busyness.

Self-Reflection Questions:

- How much of my daily activity is focused on high-impact tasks that drive my business forward?

- Do I equate busyness with productivity, and how does this affect my business growth?

- What tasks can I delegate, postpone, or eliminate to focus on activities that align with my strategic goals?

- How can I implement time management techniques to prioritise high-impact activities?

- What boundaries can I set to protect my time and focus on what truly matters?

Summary

The busyness trap is a common form of self-sabotage that creates an illusion of productivity. Business owners can spend their days filled with tasks yet make little strategic progress. To break free from this trap, it's essential to differentiate between being busy and being productive. By focusing on high-impact activities, adopting the 80/20 rule, and managing time effectively, business owners can drive meaningful results and avoid burnout. Shifting from busyness to productivity allows for strategic growth, better decision-making, and a more balanced approach to running a business.

Chapter 7:

The Comfort Zone – Avoiding Risks and Missing Opportunities

Overview

Staying within your comfort zone is a significant form of self-sabotage for many business owners. While the familiar feels safe, it often leads to stagnation and missed growth opportunities. This chapter explores why business owners avoid taking risks, the consequences of staying in their comfort zone, and how to step out and embrace calculated risks to drive progress and innovation.

Life begins when you take a step outside your comfort zone!

Understanding the Comfort Zone

- The comfort zone is a psychological state where a person feels at ease and in control of their environment. In business, this often translates to sticking with familiar routines, methods, and strategies. While it provides a sense of security, it can also create a barrier to growth. When business owners avoid stepping into the unknown, they limit their potential to explore new markets, innovate, and evolve.

- Signs You're Stuck in the Comfort Zone:

- Reluctance to try new strategies or adopt new technologies.

- Avoiding investment in new opportunities due to fear of failure.

- Sticking with the same products, services, or processes, despite a changing market.

- Making decisions based on maintaining the status quo rather than seeking growth.

Why Business Owners Avoid Risks

- Fear of Failure: One of the primary reasons business owners avoid risks is the fear of failure. Taking a risk means facing the possibility of making mistakes, losing money, or facing criticism. This fear can be paralysing, leading to inaction or reliance on what feels safe and proven.

- Overvaluation of Security: Business owners often overvalue the security of their current situation. They believe that maintaining the status quo will protect their business from downturns. However, this mindset overlooks the dynamic nature of markets, where change is constant, and inaction can be just as risky.

- Lack of Confidence: A lack of confidence in their ability to navigate new challenges can also keep business owners in their comfort zones. They may doubt their capacity to learn new skills, adapt to new environments, or recover from setbacks. This self-doubt leads to a preference for familiar territory where they feel more competent and in control.

The Consequences of Staying in the Comfort Zone

- Stagnation: By avoiding risks, businesses become stagnant. The market evolves, customer preferences change, and competitors innovate. A business that remains static in the face of these changes' risks becoming irrelevant.

- Missed Opportunities: When business owners avoid stepping out of their comfort zones, they miss out on new opportunities. Whether it's expanding into a new market, launching a new product, or adopting new technology, these opportunities often require a leap of faith.

- Limiting Business Potential: The comfort zone acts as a self-imposed ceiling on business potential. By avoiding risks, business owners limit their ability to scale, diversify, and achieve greater success. The business may perform adequately, but it will not reach its full potential.

Stepping Out of the Comfort Zone

- Reframe Failure as Learning: One of the most effective ways to overcome the fear of risk is to reframe failure. Rather than seeing it as a setback, view it as a learning experience. Every risk carries the potential for valuable insights that can inform future decisions and strategies.

- Start Small: Stepping out of the comfort zone doesn't mean taking reckless risks. Begin with small, calculated steps. Test new ideas on a small scale before fully committing. This approach minimises potential losses while allowing for learning and adjustment.

- Embrace a Growth Mindset: A growth mindset focuses on the belief that skills and abilities can be developed through dedication and hard work. By adopting this mindset, business owners can approach challenges with curiosity and resilience, viewing obstacles as opportunities to grow.

- Seek Support and Advice: Surround yourself with mentors, peers, and advisors who can provide guidance and support. Learning from others' experiences can help you assess risks more accurately and feel more confident in taking bold steps.

Practical Exercise:

The Risk-Taking Challenge

- Objective: To practice taking calculated risks and stepping out of the comfort zone in a manageable way.

- Step 1: Identify an area in your business where you've been avoiding taking a risk. This could be launching a new product, exploring a new market, investing in marketing, or implementing a new process.

- Step 2: Assess the potential risk and reward. Consider the possible outcomes, both positive and negative. What is the best-case scenario? What is the worst-case scenario? How can you mitigate the potential downsides?

- Step 3: Develop a small-scale experiment to test this risk. For example, if you're considering a new product, conduct a pilot launch or focus group to gather feedback. If exploring a new market, start with a limited marketing campaign to gauge interest.

- Step 4: Set a timeframe for the experiment and specific criteria for success. What will you measure to determine if the risk was worth taking?

- Step 5: Execute the experiment and monitor the results. Gather data and feedback to evaluate the outcomes. Reflect on what you've learned from the experience, regardless of the result.

- Outcome: This exercise encourages you to take calculated risks in a controlled environment, building confidence in your ability to step out of your comfort zone and make bold decisions.

Real-World Example:

Example: Emma's Boutique Clothing Store

Emma owned a boutique clothing store that had a steady stream of local customers. While the business was doing well, it had reached a plateau. Emma had always considered expanding her business online but feared the complexities and potential failure of e-commerce. She was comfortable with her brick-and-mortar store and hesitant to take the leap into the digital world.

Emma's Internal Struggle:

Emma feared that launching an online store would be too risky. She was concerned about the costs, the competition, and her lack of experience with e-commerce. Staying within her comfort zone felt safer, even though it limited her business's growth potential.

The Turning Point:

After attending a business networking event, Emma heard success stories from other small business owners who had expanded online. Inspired but still apprehensive, she decided to take a small step. Instead of launching a full-fledged online store, she started by selling a select range of products on an established online marketplace.

The Change:

Emma's small-scale online experiment was a success. She gained new customers and learned the basics of online retail in a low-risk environment. Encouraged by the results, she gradually expanded her online presence, eventually launching her own e-commerce website. She invested in online marketing and continued to grow her digital customer base.

Outcome:

By stepping out of her comfort zone, Emma significantly increased her revenue and expanded her brand beyond her local market. The online store not only provided a new revenue stream but also increased foot traffic to her physical store. Emma learned that taking calculated risks could open up new opportunities and drive her business forward.

Self-Reflection Questions:

- In what areas of my business am I staying within my comfort zone?

- What risks have I been avoiding due to fear of failure or uncertainty?

- How can I reframe my perception of failure as a learning opportunity?

- What small, calculated steps can I take to begin stepping out of my comfort zone?

- How can embracing risk lead to new opportunities and growth for my business?

Summary

Staying within the comfort zone may feel safe, but it often leads to stagnation and missed opportunities. Avoiding risks due to fear or a desire for security limits a business's potential to grow and evolve. By reframing failure as a learning opportunity, starting with small-scale experiments, and adopting a growth mindset, business owners can break free from their comfort zone and embrace the risks necessary for innovation and progress. Taking calculated risks is a vital part of achieving long-term success and creating a dynamic, resilient business.

CHAPTER 8:

AVOIDANCE AND PROCRASTINATION – DELAYING THE INEVITABLE

Understanding Avoidance and Procrastination

Avoidance and procrastination involve putting off tasks or decisions, especially those perceived as unpleasant, complex, or risky. It's a natural response to discomfort, but when it becomes habitual, it can significantly impact business performance. Procrastination is not about laziness; it's often rooted in deeper psychological factors such as fear, anxiety, or perfectionism.

The Psychology Behind Avoidance

Psychologically, avoidance serves as a coping mechanism. When faced with a task that triggers fear or anxiety, such as a crucial business decision or a difficult conversation with a team member, the mind seeks to protect itself by deferring action. This momentary relief from discomfort can be addictive, reinforcing the habit of avoidance. In the long term, however, this habit becomes detrimental.

Analysis Paralysis

A related concept is "analysis paralysis," where the fear of making the wrong decision leads to overthinking and inaction. Business owners may find themselves trapped in an endless loop of gathering information, weighing options, and seeking perfection, all while avoiding the actual decision.

This often results in lost opportunities and the gradual erosion of confidence in one's decision-making abilities.

Signs You're Caught in the Avoidance Trap:

- You constantly delay decisions, particularly those involving change or risk.

- You find yourself busy with low-priority tasks to avoid more critical but challenging ones.

- You feel a sense of dread when facing certain tasks, leading to distraction and postponement.

- You rationalise delays with excuses such as "I'm not ready yet" or "The timing isn't right."

Why Business Owners Procrastinate

- Fear of Failure: The fear of making the wrong decision or facing potential failure often leads to procrastination. Business owners may avoid taking action because they fear the consequences if things don't go as planned.

- Perfectionism: Perfectionism can paralyse decision-making. Business owners may delay tasks until they feel everything is perfectly aligned, leading to endless postponements and missed opportunities.

- Overwhelm: When faced with complex or daunting tasks, it's easy to feel overwhelmed. This can lead to avoidance as a means of escaping the stress associated with tackling the issue head-on.

- Lack of Clarity: Unclear goals or outcomes can cause hesitation. If the desired result or the path to achieve it is ambiguous, business owners may procrastinate rather than risk wasting time on ineffective actions.

The Costs of Avoidance and Procrastination

- Missed Opportunities: Procrastination leads to missed opportunities. Delaying important decisions can result in losing out on new markets, partnerships, or innovations that could benefit the business.

- Increased Stress and Anxiety: Avoidance doesn't eliminate the problem; it amplifies it. As the deadline looms or the issue grows, stress and anxiety increase, creating a vicious cycle that further fuels procrastination.

- Stunted Growth: Consistent avoidance hinders business growth. Critical tasks such as strategic planning, team development, and innovation are sidelined, causing the business to stagnate.

- Damaged Reputation: In some cases, avoidance can damage the business's reputation. Delaying responses to clients, avoiding difficult conversations, or failing to deliver on promises can erode trust and credibility.

Breaking Free from Avoidance

Overcoming Psychological Barriers

To break free from avoidance, it's crucial to address the psychological barriers behind it. This includes:

- Reframing Fear: Instead of seeing fear as a sign of impending failure, view it as a natural part of taking on new challenges. Fear often indicates that you are stepping out of your comfort zone, which is a necessary part of growth.

- Self-Compassion: Practice self-compassion by acknowledging that avoidance is a natural response to fear and uncertainty. Rather than criticising yourself for procrastinating, focus on what you can do differently moving forward.

Strategies to Take Action

- Break Tasks into Smaller Steps: Large tasks can be overwhelming. Break them down into smaller, more manageable steps. By focusing on one step at a time, you reduce the sense of overwhelm and make progress more achievable.

- Set Clear Priorities: Prioritise tasks based on their importance and impact. Use tools like the Eisenhower Matrix to distinguish between urgent and important tasks, ensuring that high-priority items receive the attention they deserve.

- Set Deadlines and Commit: Set specific deadlines for completing tasks and commit to them. Deadlines create a sense of urgency and accountability, helping to overcome the tendency to delay.

- Adopt the Two-Minute Rule: If a task takes two minutes or less, do it immediately. This simple rule helps prevent small tasks from piling up and becoming sources of stress.

- Use Accountability Partners: Share your goals and deadlines with a trusted colleague, mentor, or coach. An accountability partner can provide support, encouragement, and a gentle push when procrastination creeps in.

- Implement Time-Blocking: Use time-blocking to dedicate specific times of the day to high-priority tasks. This helps create a structured approach to tackling important tasks without allowing them to be overshadowed by distractions.

Overcoming Setbacks

Even with the best intentions, there may be times when avoidance resurfaces. When setbacks occur:

- Reflect Without Judgment: Reflect on what triggered the avoidance. Was it fear, uncertainty, or overwhelm? Use this insight to adjust your approach moving forward.

- Revisit Your Action Plan: If avoidance has caused a delay, revisit your action plan. Break the task into even smaller steps if needed and take the first step immediately to regain momentum.

Practical Exercise:

The Action Plan Accelerator

- Objective: To overcome procrastination by creating an actionable plan for tackling a task or decision you've been avoiding.

- Step 1: Identify a task or decision you've been avoiding. It could be anything from making a significant business decision to addressing a performance issue with a team member.

- Step 2: Break the task into smaller, manageable steps. List each step, no matter how small, in sequential order.

- Step 3: Set a deadline for each step. Make sure the deadlines are realistic but also create a sense of urgency to prompt action.

- Step 4: Address the underlying fear. Write down the fears or concerns that have caused you to avoid this task. Challenge these fears by asking, "What's the worst that can happen?" and "How can I mitigate the risks?"

- Step 5: Find an Accountability Partner. Share your action plan with a trusted colleague or mentor who can provide encouragement and hold you accountable.

- Step 6: Take the first step. Commit to taking the first action on your list immediately. Often, starting the process helps overcome the inertia of procrastination.

- Step 7: Reflect on the outcome. Once you complete the task, reflect on the experience. Did the fears materialise? How did taking action impact your stress levels and progress?

- Outcome: This exercise encourages you to confront avoidance by breaking tasks into manageable steps and taking immediate action. It builds momentum and confidence, reducing the tendency to procrastinate in the future.

Real-World Example:

Example: James's Digital Marketing Agency

James owned a digital marketing agency that was growing rapidly. However, he avoided making decisions about hiring new staff to handle the increased workload. He feared that hiring the wrong people would result in financial loss and negatively affect his agency's reputation. As a result, James took on more work himself, becoming increasingly overwhelmed.

James's Internal Struggle:

James feared that expanding his team was a risk he couldn't afford. He worried about the financial implications and the potential impact on client satisfaction. His avoidance led to long hours, stress, and declining performance, both personally and within his agency.

The Turning Point:

After realising he couldn't maintain the current workload without sacrificing quality, James decided to confront his avoidance. He created an action plan that included defining the roles he needed to fill, setting a hiring budget, and creating a timeline for the hiring process. James also sought advice from a mentor who helped him see the long-term benefits of expanding his team.

The Change:

James broke down the hiring process into smaller steps: drafting job descriptions, posting job ads, reviewing applications, and conducting interviews. He set clear deadlines for each step and started with the first action—writing the job descriptions. By focusing on one small task at a time, James was able to move past his fear of the larger process. He also implemented feedback from his mentor, which helped him fine-tune his approach to hiring and made him feel more confident in the process.

The Outcome:

James successfully hired two new team members, allowing him to delegate tasks and focus on high-impact activities. The new hires brought fresh ideas and expertise, enhancing the agency's service offerings. As a result, the agency began attracting larger clients and expanding its reach. James realised that his avoidance had been holding his business back. By taking decisive action, he not only alleviated his own stress but also positioned his agency for further growth. The experience taught him that while taking action might involve some risk, the cost of avoidance was far greater in the long term.

Self-Reflection Questions:

- What tasks or decisions have I been avoiding in my business, and why?

- How do my fears or concerns contribute to my avoidance behaviour?

- What small steps can I take today to start addressing these tasks?

- How does avoiding action impact my business's growth and my stress levels?

- What support or resources can I use to help overcome procrastination and take action?

Summary

Avoidance and procrastination are common yet detrimental behaviours that can significantly hinder business growth. By delaying critical tasks and decisions, business owners miss out on opportunities and create larger problems.

Overcoming avoidance involves acknowledging the behaviour, breaking tasks into smaller steps, setting clear priorities, and committing to action. By taking decisive steps, you can reduce stress, gain momentum, and drive your business forward.

The key is to confront avoidance directly, understand its underlying causes, and take proactive measures to move past it.

The job you never start takes
the longest time to finish

Chapter 9:

The Absence of Clear Goals – Drifting Without Direction

Overview

A lack of clear goals is one of the most significant ways business owners sabotage their progress. Without a defined direction, businesses drift aimlessly, reacting to circumstances rather than proactively shaping their future. This chapter explores the importance of setting clear, achievable goals, the pitfalls of operating without them, and strategies to establish a goal-driven framework that propels the business toward success.

The Importance of Clear Goals

- Clear goals serve as the roadmap for a business's journey. They provide direction, focus, and a basis for measuring progress. Without them, efforts become scattered, and the business operates in a reactive mode rather than a strategic one. Goals give purpose to daily activities, aligning efforts with the larger vision and ensuring that every action contributes to the overall objectives.

- Key Benefits of Clear Goals:

  - Direction: Goals define where you want your business to go and how you plan to get there.

- Motivation: Having clear goals provides motivation and a sense of purpose for both the business owner and the team.

- Accountability: Goals create benchmarks for success, allowing for accountability and performance evaluation.

- Decision-Making: Clear goals simplify decision-making by serving as a filter to determine which opportunities align with the business's desired path.

Signs Your Business Lacks Clear Goals

- Reactive Operations: You find yourself constantly reacting to problems and market changes without a long-term strategy.

- Inconsistent Progress: Your business experiences sporadic growth with no clear trajectory or pattern.

- Overwhelm and Confusion: Without clear goals, it's easy to feel overwhelmed by the multitude of tasks and decisions that arise daily.

- Lack of Team Alignment: Your team is uncertain about the business's priorities, leading to a lack of focus and cohesive effort.

The Consequences of Drifting Without Goals

- Wasted Resources: Without clear goals, time, money, and effort are often wasted on activities that don't contribute to growth or long-term success. Business owners may invest in initiatives that seem urgent but don't align with a strategic vision, resulting in a cycle of inefficiency.

- Stagnation: A lack of goals leads to stagnation. Without a target to aim for, the business is likely to plateau, lacking the drive and innovation needed for continuous growth.

- Decreased Morale: Employees thrive on purpose and direction. When a business lacks clear goals, it leads to confusion and disengagement among the team, reducing productivity and morale.

- Missed Opportunities: Clear goals enable proactive behaviour and readiness to seize opportunities that align with the business's direction. Without them, potential growth opportunities often go unnoticed or are acted upon too late.

Establishing a Goal-Driven Framework

- Set SMART Goals: Use the SMART criteria (Specific, Measurable, Achievable, Relevant, Time-bound) to define clear goals. SMART goals are detailed and structured, providing a clear pathway for action and measurement.

- Break Down Goals into Actionable Steps: Large goals can be daunting. Break them down into smaller, manageable tasks and milestones to maintain momentum and track progress. This process makes the path to achieving the goal less overwhelming and more attainable.

- Align Goals with Vision and Values: Goals should align with the broader vision and values of the business. This alignment ensures that every objective contributes to the long-term aspirations of the business and resonates with its core values.

- Regular Review and Adaptation: Goals are not static. Regularly review your progress and be willing to adapt as circumstances change. This flexibility allows you to stay on track even when external factors impact your original plans.

Practical Exercise:

Goal-Setting Blueprint

- Objective: To develop clear, actionable goals for your business that align with your long-term vision.

- Step 1: Identify the key areas of your business that need improvement or growth (e.g., revenue, customer base, product development).

- Step 2: For each area, set a SMART goal. Ensure each goal is specific, measurable, achievable, relevant, and time-bound. For example, "Increase monthly revenue by 20% within six months through the launch of a new product line."

- Step 3: Break each goal into smaller, actionable steps. Create a timeline for completing each step, assigning responsibilities and setting deadlines.

- Step 4: Align each goal with your business's vision and values. Ask yourself how achieving each goal contributes to the bigger picture and what impact it will have on your business's future.

- Step 5: Implement a regular review process. Set a schedule to review your progress towards each goal (e.g., monthly or quarterly). Use these reviews to assess what's working, identify challenges, and adjust your strategies if necessary.

- Outcome: This exercise provides a structured approach to setting and pursuing clear, actionable goals that align with your business's vision. It helps you move from a state of drifting to one of focused, strategic action.

Real-World Example:

Example: Rachel's Home Décor Business

Rachel ran a home décor business with a small but loyal customer base. While her business was steady, it wasn't growing as she had hoped. She realised that she lacked clear goals and was simply reacting to day-to-day demands without a strategic direction.

Rachel's Internal Struggle:

Rachel was caught in a cycle of busyness without progress. She worked hard every day but felt she was merely maintaining the status quo. Her marketing efforts were sporadic, and she often felt overwhelmed by the multitude of tasks she faced. Without clear goals, she found it difficult to prioritise her actions and make decisions that would drive growth.

The Turning Point:

After attending a business planning workshop, Rachel recognised the importance of setting clear, measurable goals. She decided to create a goal-setting framework for her business. She started by defining her long-term vision: to become a leading provider of unique, sustainable home décor in her region. With this vision in mind, she set specific goals, such as increasing her online sales by 30% within a year and expanding her product line to include eco-friendly options.

The Change:

Rachel broke down her goals into actionable steps. For example, to increase online sales, she focused on improving her website, launching targeted marketing campaigns, and enhancing her customer service experience. She set monthly milestones to track her progress and adapted her strategies based on her reviews. By aligning her daily activities with her long-term goals, Rachel found a renewed sense of purpose and direction in her business.

Outcome:

Within a year, Rachel's home décor business experienced significant growth. Her online sales increased by 35%, surpassing her initial goal. The introduction of eco-friendly products attracted a new customer segment and differentiated her brand in the market. Rachel learned that having clear goals gave her a roadmap to follow, making her efforts more focused and effective. She moved from a reactive state to a proactive, goal-driven approach that propelled her business forward.

Self-Reflection Questions:

- Do I have clear, specific goals for my business, or am I drifting without direction?

- How do my daily activities align with my long-term vision and goals?

- What are the key areas in my business that need clear goals to drive growth and progress?

- How can I break down my larger goals into smaller, actionable steps?

- How often do I review and adapt my goals to ensure they remain relevant and achievable?

Summary

The absence of clear goals leaves businesses drifting without direction, reacting to circumstances rather than proactively pursuing a defined path. Setting SMART goals provides the roadmap needed for growth, accountability, and strategic decision-making.

By breaking down larger goals into actionable steps, aligning them with the business's vision, and regularly reviewing progress, business owners can shift from a state of stagnation to one of purposeful, goal-driven action.

Clarity in goals fosters motivation, alignment, and progress, creating a business that is focused, agile, and primed for success.

CHAPTER 10:

BUILDING A BUSINESS THAT RUNS WITHOUT YOU – THE PATH TO FREEDOM – TIME TO REFLECT

Overview

The ultimate goal for many business owners is to create a business that operates independently, allowing them to step back and enjoy the freedom they've worked hard to achieve. However, getting to this point requires overcoming self-sabotage and implementing systems and strategies that foster autonomy and growth. In this final chapter, we'll explore the steps necessary to build a business that runs without you, ensuring long-term sustainability and success.

The Importance of an Independent Business

- A business that can run without the constant involvement of its owner is not only more sustainable but also more valuable. It allows the owner to focus on strategic growth, explore new ventures, or simply enjoy a better work-life balance. Independence also ensures that the business can thrive even if the owner decides to take a break, sell, or retire.

- Key Benefits of an Independent Business:

  - Scalability: A business that doesn't rely on the owner for daily operations can scale more effectively.

- Increased Value: Businesses that can operate independently are often more attractive to buyers, increasing their market value.

- Work-Life Balance: Owners gain the freedom to step back, knowing that the business can sustain itself without their constant oversight.

The Self-Sabotage Barrier to Independence

- Fear of Losing Control: Many owners fear that letting go will result in a decline in quality or standards. This fear leads to micromanagement, making it difficult for the business to operate without the owner's involvement.

- Over-Reliance on the Owner: When the owner is involved in every aspect of the business, it becomes dependent on their presence. This over-reliance creates a bottleneck that hinders growth and independence.

- Lack of Systems and Processes: A common barrier to independence is the absence of well-defined systems and processes. Without them, the business cannot function smoothly without the owner's direct input.

Steps to Building an Independent Business

- Develop Systems and Processes: Establish clear, documented systems and processes for every aspect of your business. This includes operations, customer service, marketing, and finance. Well-documented processes ensure that tasks can be carried out consistently and efficiently, even in your absence.

- Empower Your Team: Empowering your team means delegating responsibilities and trusting them to make decisions. Invest in training and development to ensure they have the skills and confidence to operate autonomously. Encourage a culture of accountability where team members take ownership of their roles.

- Create a Strong Leadership Structure: A business that can run without the owner needs a strong leadership team. Identify key roles within the business and assign responsibilities to capable leaders who can oversee day-to-day operations. This leadership structure provides stability and direction, reducing the need for the owner's constant involvement.

- Automate Where Possible: Implement automation tools to handle repetitive tasks. Automation not only increases efficiency but also reduces the likelihood of errors. From customer relationship management (CRM) systems to automated billing, leverage technology to streamline operations.

- Establish Clear KPIs and Reporting: Define Key Performance Indicators (KPIs) that measure the success of various aspects of your business. Implement regular reporting systems to monitor these KPIs, allowing you to stay informed about the business's performance without being directly involved in every detail.

- Plan for Contingencies: Develop contingency plans to handle potential crises or unexpected events. This includes having a succession plan in place, ensuring that there are clear procedures for dealing with disruptions. A robust contingency plan ensures the business can continue to operate smoothly in the owner's absence.

Maintaining Independence Over Time

- Regular Review and Improvement: Regularly review your systems, processes, and team performance to identify areas for improvement. Independence is not a one-time achievement but an ongoing process that requires adjustment and refinement.

- Step Back Gradually: Test the independence of your business by gradually stepping back. Start by taking short breaks and monitor how the business performs. Gradually increase the duration of your absence, allowing your team to adapt and grow in confidence.

- Shift Your Role: Transition your role from being involved in daily operations to focusing on strategic growth. Your focus should shift to guiding the long-term vision, exploring new opportunities, and mentoring your leadership team.

Practical Exercise:

The Independence Blueprint

- Objective: To create a step-by-step plan for building a business that can operate independently of the owner.

- Step 1: Identify Core Operations: List the core operations of your business that require your direct involvement.

Identify which of these can be systematised, delegated, or automated.

- Step 2: Develop Systems and Processes: For each core operation, create detailed, step-by-step processes. Document these processes clearly, including checklists, templates, and guidelines.

- Step 3: Delegate Responsibilities: Identify team members who can take on specific responsibilities. Provide training and support to ensure they are equipped to handle these tasks autonomously.

- Step 4: Implement Automation: Explore automation tools that can streamline repetitive tasks. Implement these tools and integrate them into your business processes.

- Step 5: Establish a Leadership Structure: Develop a clear organisational structure with defined roles and responsibilities. Empower your leadership team to oversee operations and make decisions.

- Step 6: Create a Monitoring System: Establish KPIs and a reporting system to monitor the performance of your business. Set up regular meetings with your leadership team to review performance and address any issues.

- Step 7: Test the Independence: Gradually step back from daily operations. Start with short breaks, and progressively increase the duration of your absence to test how well the business operates without you.

- Outcome: This exercise helps you systematically create a business that can run independently, enabling you to step back and focus on strategic growth or personal pursuits.

Real-World Example:

Example: Tom's Tech Solutions

Tom owned a tech solutions company that he had built from the ground up. As the business grew, he found himself increasingly involved in every aspect, from client interactions to technical troubleshooting. While Tom loved his work, he realised that the business was entirely dependent on him, limiting its potential for growth and putting his well-being at risk.

Tom's Internal Struggle:

Tom feared that stepping back would result in a decline in service quality. He believed that his clients relied on his expertise and that delegating key responsibilities would compromise the business's reputation. However, the constant involvement was taking a toll on his health and personal life

The Turning Point:

Tom decided it was time to create a business that could operate without his daily input. He began by identifying the core operations that required his involvement and documented detailed processes for each. He then worked on building a strong leadership team, promoting experienced staff members to manage different departments.

The Change:

Tom invested in training for his team, empowering them to take ownership of their roles. He also implemented automation tools for routine tasks such as customer support and billing. To monitor the business's performance, Tom established KPIs and a regular reporting system. He started by taking short breaks, gradually increasing the length of his absences.

Outcome:

Over time, Tom's business began to run smoothly without his direct involvement. The leadership team managed daily operations, and automated systems handled routine tasks. Tom shifted his focus to strategic growth and exploring new market opportunities. The business continued to thrive, and Tom gained the freedom to take extended breaks without worrying about its day-to-day operations. By building a business that could run independently, Tom not only improved his quality of life but also increased the value and scalability of his company.

Self-Reflection Questions:

- What areas of my business currently rely heavily on my direct involvement?

- How can I develop systems and processes to reduce this reliance?

- Who on my team can take on more responsibility, and what support do they need to succeed?

- What steps can I take to gradually step back and test the independence of my business?

- How will building a business that can operate without me impact my work-life balance and long-term vision?

Summary

Building a business that can run without the owner's constant involvement is the ultimate goal for creating freedom, scalability, and long-term success. It requires overcoming self-sabotage, developing clear systems and processes, empowering a capable team, and implementing automation and monitoring systems.

By gradually stepping back and shifting focus to strategic growth, business owners can enjoy the benefits of a self-sustaining enterprise that thrives in their absence. The journey to independence is a path to true business freedom, enabling owners to achieve both personal and professional fulfilment.

It is time to work ON your business, not just IN it!

Recap Key Lessons

Let's revisit each of the key lessons with some added depth and practical insights. The idea here is not just to summarise but to drive home how these lessons fit together like puzzle pieces:

1. Awareness: Most business owners wear their busyness like a badge of honour, but it's actually the first red flag. Being "too busy" often means being too blind to see the bigger picture. We discussed how crucial it is to step back regularly—whether through quarterly reviews, mentorship, or simply scheduled reflection times. Awareness isn't just the first step; it's the ongoing practice of recognising when you're slipping back into old habits.

2. Delegation: We had dived into the fear behind delegation. It's not just about handing off tasks; it's about trusting others to carry a piece of your vision. Remember Jane's story from Chapter 2? She was so ingrained in her daily tasks that her business couldn't grow without her. When she finally took the leap to delegate even small responsibilities, her team stepped up, and she discovered talents within her business that she never knew existed.

3. Systems and Processes: Chaos feels like action, but it's just masked inefficiency. The power of systems is in their simplicity. Think of the McDonald's model—systems so

foolproof that anyone can step in and run a store. Your business needs its own "Operations Bible." It's not about over-engineering things; it's about creating repeatable processes that free you to focus on growth. Remember, each time you document a process, you're buying back a piece of your freedom.

4. Mindset Shift: Moving from doer to leader isn't an overnight switch; it's a gradual change in how you view your role. Leaders don't just give orders; they inspire a vision. Your mindset shift might start with small things like leading team meetings with a focus on collaboration rather than control. Each moment you choose to guide rather than dictate is a step toward building a team that functions without constant oversight.

5. Financial Intelligence: We spent an entire chapter unpacking the importance of understanding your financials. It's not about becoming an accountant but about becoming financially literate enough to make informed decisions. Profit margins, cash flow, ROI—these aren't just numbers; they're the lifeblood of your business. The more you understand them, the more control you have over your business's destiny.

6. Work-Life Balance: This is the antidote to burnout. In the hustle to build a business, it's easy to forget why you started

in the first place. Remember the example of Mark, who was running on fumes until he finally prioritised balance? That simple shift led to more creative thinking, better decision-making, and a business that didn't consume his entire life.

7. Adaptability: Change is the only constant in business. The companies that survive and thrive are those that adapt. Your business needs to be a living, breathing organism capable of evolving with market demands, technological advances, and shifts in consumer behaviour. It's not about abandoning what works but about staying ahead of what comes next.

8. Goal Setting and Planning: Goals are your North Star. Without them, you're drifting. It's not just about setting goals but about setting the right goals—ones that align with the ultimate vision of a self-sustaining business. This includes not just revenue targets but also goals related to team development, process optimisation, and personal growth.

9. Continuous Learning: Stagnation is the silent killer of businesses. What you knew five years ago may not be enough today. Commit to being a perpetual student. Whether it's reading industry reports, attending seminars, or learning from mentors, staying ahead means always being open to new knowledge.

10. Self-Reflection: This final piece is about checking in with yourself regularly. The business landscape changes, your team changes, and so do you. Self-reflection keeps you aligned with your goals and ensures you're not veering off course. It's the habit that ties all other lessons together, ensuring you remain on a path of growth and freedom.

Next Steps - Detailed Action Plan

You've got the theory; now let's turn it into action. Here's a step-by-step plan, broken down into manageable chunks, that will guide you on this journey:

1. Self-Audit: Set aside a full day for a comprehensive self-audit. Analyse your daily routines, identify tasks you handle that could be delegated, and pinpoint processes that lack clarity. Document these findings. This isn't a cursory glance; it's a deep dive into your habits and business operations. Your goal is to unearth every area where self-sabotage has taken root.

2. Delegate One Task: Choose one task that you handle regularly but doesn't require your unique skill set. Begin with something low-risk if it makes you nervous. For instance, delegate the task of scheduling meetings or managing social media updates. Train the person taking over the task, provide clear guidelines, and most importantly, let go. Trust the process and be prepared to see surprising results.

3. Build One System: Look at one chaotic aspect of your business. Is it the onboarding process for new clients? The way you handle customer complaints. Start with one process and map it out. Develop a simple, repeatable system, whether it's a flowchart, a checklist, or an SOP

(Standard Operating Procedure). Pilot this system and refine it as needed. The goal here is progress, not perfection.

4. Set One New Goal: Goals drive focus. Set one specific, measurable, and achievable goal for the next quarter. For example, your goal might be to increase customer retention by 10% by the end of the quarter. Break this goal down into actionable steps. Share this goal with your team and involve them in the planning process. Their buy-in is crucial for success.

5. Schedule Downtime: Right now, open your calendar and block out time for yourself. Not just a single evening but a regular weekly slot. Use this time for activities that recharge you, whether that's spending time with family, pursuing a hobby, or simply doing nothing. This is non-negotiable. Remember, a burnt-out leader can't lead.

6. Learn and Reflect: Establish a monthly learning and reflection session. Use this time to review your progress, assess what's working, and identify areas for improvement. Keep a journal of these reflections. This practice will help you stay aware of your journey and ensure you're continually growing.

Long-Term Vision

Imagine the ripple effect of these changes. In the long term, you're not just building a business; you're building a legacy. A business that works without you doesn't mean you're irrelevant; it means you've succeeded in creating something greater than yourself. Here's what this vision could look like:

- Improved Work-Life Balance: You have time to enjoy your success. This means more moments with family, hobbies, travel, or simply the peace of knowing you can step away without everything falling apart. You're not just surviving; you're thriving.

- Increased Business Value: A business that runs independently is inherently more valuable. Investors and buyers are drawn to businesses that don't hinge on the owner's daily involvement. You're building an asset that can be sold, expanded, or franchised, multiplying its value.

- Resilience: Your business becomes robust and capable of withstanding market shifts, economic downturns, and industry changes. You've created a team and systems that adapt and pivot without requiring you to be in the trenches every day.

- Legacy: You leave behind more than just a business—you leave a legacy. Whether that's a brand known for excellence, a team empowered to innovate, or a business model others aspire to emulate, your impact lasts beyond your active involvement.

Be stubborn on the long-term vision, but flexible on the details [Jeff Bezos]

"Head Down, Balls Up"

With your 'head down' in your work and no 'looking ahead' the chances of error through a lack of foresight, strategy and getting out of your own way means a 'balls up' is much more likely.

So here we are. If you've made it to this point, congratulations—you've managed to stick with it, which means there's hope for you yet! But let's get something straight: reading this book isn't enough. Knowing you're prone to self-sabotage is only the beginning. Like knowing you're overweight and still going for that second slice of cake—awareness alone won't fix it. You need ACTION.

If there's one thing I want you to take away from all of this, it's that the *work* that matters isn't more busy work. It's the uncomfortable, unsexy stuff that we love to avoid. It's the conversations with your team you've been putting off, the delegation you've been dodging, and the strategies you've been overthinking to death. It's time to stop glorifying the hustle and start embracing what it truly means to be a business owner—someone who builds systems, empowers people, and ultimately creates a business that can thrive without you glued to it.

Now, I can already hear some of you protesting: "But I'm different! My business is special! No one can do it like I do!" Guess what? That's exactly the mindset that's holding you back. Your job isn't to be the hero who swoops in and saves the day. Your job is to make sure the day doesn't need saving in the first place.

By now, you should be able to spot the signs of self-sabotage in your behaviour: procrastination, perfectionism, overthinking, and that classic martyr syndrome where you're convinced the whole business will crumble if you take a day off. Spoiler alert: it won't. If it does, then congratulations—you've built a job, not a business. That's not freedom, that's a gilded prison cage.

So what's next? Well, that's up to you. You can either carry on the way you have been—grinding, hustling, firefighting your way through every day—or you can start making the changes that will free you from the hamster wheel. You've got the roadmap now. The question is, do you have the guts to follow it?

If you're serious about creating a **commercial, profitable enterprise that works without you**, then it's time to get your head out of the ground and make it happen. Because if you don't, you'll be here a year from now, reading another business book, wondering why nothing has changed. And honestly? That's the real tragedy.

So, what's it going to be? More Head Down, Balls Up? More work and busyness and more errors and lack of growth?

OR

Time for a change, in you!

Accountability

Let's face it—change is daunting. But here's the truth: The only way to achieve a different outcome is to take different actions. You have the blueprint in your hands. The next steps are up to you. In the words of Rita Mae Brown:

> *"Insanity is doing the same thing over and over again and expecting different results"*

You're not alone on this journey. Every successful entrepreneur has faced the same fears, the same hurdles, and the same internal battles. The difference between those who succeed and those who don't is simple: ACTION.

You've invested time in reading this book. Now, invest that time in yourself and your business. Start with one small change. Delegate that task. Build that system. Take that day off. Each action, no matter how small, is a step away from self-sabotage and a step toward freedom.

Lastly, who is your accountability partner? Who is that person who will question you, hold you to account and be a royal pain in the backside? If you have nobody to do that you are missing a trick, message me directly at saboteur@simonellson.com and I will help to keep you on track.

The question now is: Will you let this book be just another read, or will it be the catalyst for your transformation? The power is in your hands.

Make the choice. Make it count - Your business and your life are waiting.

"Whether you think you can, or think you can't, you're right"

[Henry Ford]

About the Author

Simon Ellson is a results-oriented business coach, a straight-talking entrepreneur, and a firm believer in building businesses that work *without* their owners glued to them. With over two decades of experience coaching everyone from ambitious startups to seasoned business leaders, and over 40 years in business, building companies of his own. Simon knows exactly what it takes to transform a business from chaotic to controlled.

Simon's favourite quote, "You don't know what you don't know" which leads to lifelong learning!

As the founder of the Complete Coaching Practice in both Dorset and Hertfordshire, Simon has made it his mission to help business owners not just survive but thrive. His 121 coaching and his specialised 12-week programmes on Management, Sales, Leadership, and Business have become the go-to for entrepreneurs looking to make more profit, build better teams, and—most importantly—find a little breathing room in their work-life balance.

Known for his sunny attitude, dry humour and no-BS approach, Simon regularly coaches 30 to 40 business owners, helping them get out of their own way and back in control of their businesses. Simon will also help you get buyer-ready and to sell your business if that is your end goal.

Having served his time in large corporates, Apple and Symantec, he decided entrepreneurship was the place he loved the most and coaching has been a logical extension of that.

When he's not coaching, Simon is an avid Formula 1 and Rugby fan. He's been happily married to his wife Viv for over 35 years, and they have six wonderful grandchildren.

This book is dedicated to his three children—Seb, Ed, and Tim—their partners, all his grandchildren, and, of course, his wife Viv, who has truly been his partner in every way since the day they first met.

Simon also pays tribute to two important gentlemen in his life: his father Roger, who passed away when Simon was just thirteen, and his uncle Tim, a successful business owner himself who played a crucial role in Simon's early years and became a massive inspiration, sadly no longer with us.

For more insights, and perhaps a dry quip or two, you can always connect with Simon and his team on LinkedIn at linkedin.com/in/sellson, where he regularly shares his thoughts on leadership, business, and life in the fast lane.

NOTE: Resources, diagrams and useful PDF's relating to the content of this book are always available at https://simonellson.com

Printed in Dunstable, United Kingdom

67533921R00068